# World Languages

# Colours in French

## Daniel Nunn

D0257806

**www.raintreepublishers.co.uk**
Visit our website to find out
more information about
Raintree books.

**To order:**
☎ Phone 0845 6044371
📄 Fax +44 (0) 1865 312263
💻 Email myorders@raintreepublishers.co.uk

Customers from outside the UK please telephone +44 1865 312262

Raintree is an imprint of Capstone Global Library Limited,
a company incorporated in England and Wales having its
registered office at 7 Pilgrim Street, London, EC4V 6LB
– Registered company number: 6695582

Text © Capstone Global Library Limited 2013
First published in hardback in 2013
First published in paperback in 2013
The moral rights of the proprietor have been asserted.

Edited by Daniel Nunn, Rebecca Rissman, and Sian Smith
Designed by Joanna Hinton-Malivoire
Picture research by Elizabeth Alexander
Production by Alison Parsons
Originated by Capstone Global Library Ltd
Printed in China

ISBN 978 1 406 23918 8 (hardback)
16 15 14 13 12
10 9 8 7 6 5 4 3 2 1

ISBN 978 1 406 23925 6 (paperback)
17 16 15 14 13
10 9 8 7 6 5 4 3 2 1

**British Library Cataloguing in Publication Data**
Nunn, Daniel.
  Colours in French. -- (World languages. Colours)
  1. French language--Vocabulary--Juvenile literature.
  2. Colors--Juvenile literature. 3. French language--
  Textbooks for foreign speakers--English.
  I. Title II. Series
  448.2'421-dc23

**Acknowledgements**
We would like to thank Shutterstock for permission to reproduce pho-
tographs: pp.4 (© Phiseksit), 5 (© Stephen Aaron Rees), 6 (© Tischenko
Irina), 7 (© Tony Magdaraog), 8 (© szefei), 9 (© Picsfive), 10 (© Eric
Isselée), 11 (© Yasonya), 12 (© Nadezhda Bolotina), 13 (© Maryna
Gviazdovska), 14 (© Erik Lam), 15 (© Eric Isselée), 16 (© Ruth Black),
17 (© blueskies9), 18 (© Alexander Dashewsky), 19 (© Michele
Perbellini), 20 (© Eric Isselée), 21 (© Roman Rvachov).

Cover photographs reproduced with permission of Shutterstock: dog
(© Erik Lam), strawberry (© Stephen Aaron Rees), fish (© Tischenko
Irina). Back cover photograph of a parrot reproduced with permission
of Shutterstock (© Eric Isselée ).

We would like to thank... for their help in
the preparation of...

Every effort has been made to contact copyright holders of material
reproduced in this book. Any omissions will be rectified in subsequent
printings if notice is given to the publisher.

# Contents

# Rouge

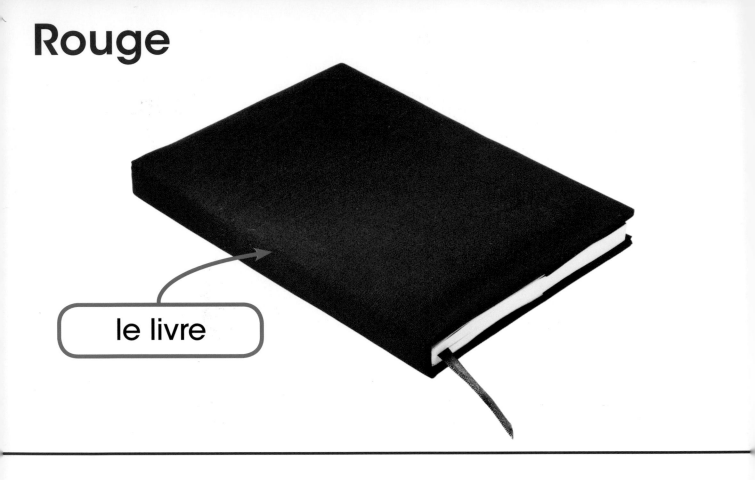

le livre

Le livre est rouge.

The book is red.

la fraise

La fraise est rouge.

The strawberry is red.

# Orange

le poisson

Le poisson est orange.

The fish is orange.

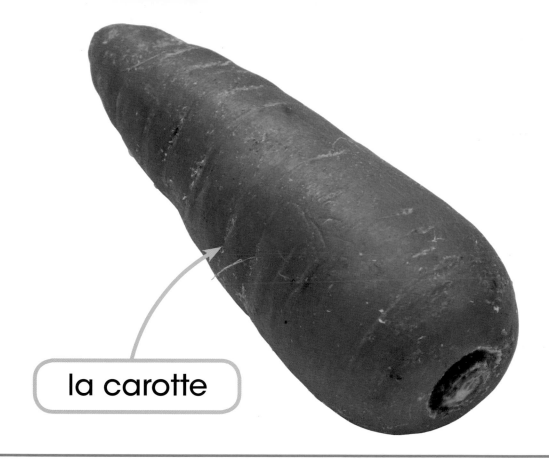

la carotte

La carotte est orange.

The carrot is orange.

# Jaune

la fleur

La fleur est jaune.

The flower is yellow.

La banane est jaune.

The banana is yellow.

# Vert

l'oiseau

L'oiseau est vert.

The bird is green.

la pomme

La pomme est verte.

The apple is green.

# Bleu

le T-shirt

Le T-shirt est bleu.

The T-shirt is blue.

la tasse

La tasse est bleue.

The cup is blue.

# Marron

le chien

Le chien est marron.

The dog is brown.

la vache

La vache est marron.

The cow is brown.

# Rose

le gâteau

Le gâteau est rose.

The cake is pink.

le chapeau

Le chapeau est rose.

The hat is pink.

# Blanc

le lait

Le lait est blanc.

The milk is white.

la neige

La neige est blanche.

The snow is white.

# Noir

le chat

Le chat est **noir**.

The cat is **black**.

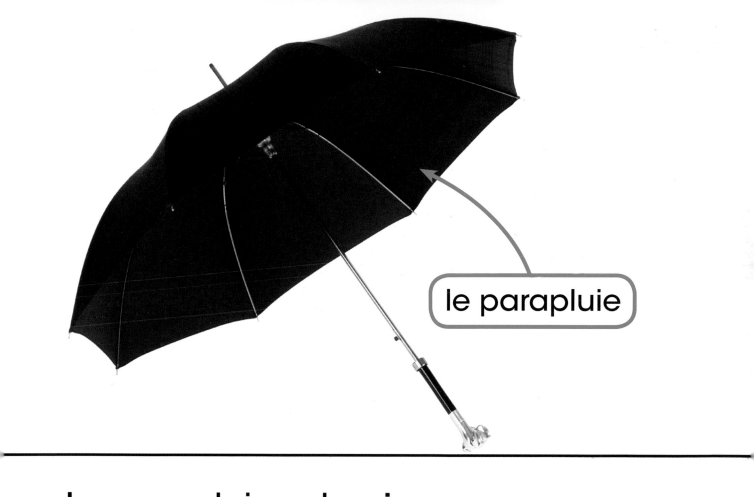

le parapluie

Le parapluie est **noir**.

The umbrella is **black**.

# Dictionary

| French word | How to say it | English word |
|---|---|---|
| banane | ba-nan | banana |
| blanc/blanche | blon/blonsh | white |
| bleu/bleue | bluh/bluh | blue |
| carotte | ka-rot | carrot |
| chapeau | shap-oh | hat |
| chat | cha | cat |
| chien | che-an | dog |
| est | ay | is |
| fleur | flur | flower |
| fraise | frayz | strawberry |
| gâteau | ga-tow | cake |
| jaune | jone | yellow |
| la | la | the |
| lait | lay | milk |
| le | luh | the |
| livre | leevre | book |

| French word | How to say it | English word |
|---|---|---|
| marron | ma-ron | brown |
| neige | nehj | snow |
| noir | nwoir | black |
| oiseau | wa-zo | bird |
| orange | or-onj | orange |
| parapluie | pa-ra-plwee | umbrella |
| poisson | pwo-sohn | fish |
| pomme | pom | apple |
| rose | rohz | pink |
| rouge | rooj | red |
| T-shirt | tee-shirt | T-shirt |
| tasse | tas | cup |
| vache | vash | cow |
| vert/verte | vair/vairt | green |

See words in the "How to say it" columns for a rough guide to pronunciations.

# Index

**Notes for parents and teachers**

In French, nouns are either masculine or feminine. The word for "the" changes accordingly – either le (masculine) or la (feminine). Sometimes adjectives have different spellings too, depending on whether the noun is masculine or feminine. This is why some of the colours have more than one spelling.